Mixed Media

Deri Robins

MINNETONKA, MINNESOTA

This edition published in 2006 in North America by
Two-Can Publishing
11571 K-Tel Drive
Minnetonka, MN 55343
www.two-canpublishing.com

Two-Can wishes to thank artist Shannon Steven for
her help with the American terms in this book.

Library of Congress CIP data on file

ISBN 1-58728-545-2

Written by Deri Robins
Designed by Wladek Szechter/Louise Morley
Edited by Sian Morgan/Matthew Harvey
Photographer: Michael Wicks
Thanks to Nicola

Creative Director: Louise Morley
Editorial Manager: Jean Coppendale

Printed and bound in China

1 2 3 4 5 10 09 08 07 06

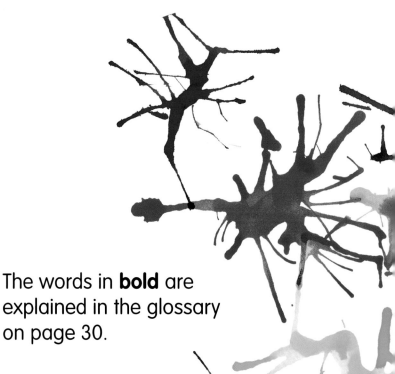

The words in **bold** are
explained in the glossary
on page 30.

Contents

Tools and materials   4
Hints and tips   6
Straw painting   8
Dripping and dabbing   10
Wax resist   12
Scratchboard   14
Wax transfer   16
Glitter project   18
Fabric collage   20
Paper sewing   22
Collage   24
Extra materials   26
Using photos   28
Glossary   30
Index   31
Notes to parents and teachers   32

Tools and materials

This book is about creating fascinating and unusual art using a variety of tools and materials. None of the materials are expensive or hard to find, and those shown on these pages should enable you to try most of the projects in the book.

wax crayons

Paints

You can make poster paints as thin or thick as you like, so they are ideal for many special effects (see pages 8–15).

Crayons

A number of the art projects use wax crayons (see pages 12–17). If you don't have a white crayon, you can use a white candle instead.

Inks

You can get amazing effects using inks, with both dry and wet paper. Try using waterproof inks.

Paper

Try a variety of papers. Thick paper or card stock is better for watery paint, because it is less likely to buckle. **Collages** need cardboard for a base. Paper towels or blotting paper, as well as parchment paper, tissue paper, construction paper, and **textured** paper are all useful.

Tools and brushes

Ordinary brushes are useful for details and for paint washes, but you may want some more unusual tools, too. Straws are good for making bubble prints, for blowing paint, and for making paper curls. Anything with a sharp point, such as a knitting needle or toothpick, is good for scratchboard pictures or wax transfers. Scissors and glue are essential for collages.

Extra materials

Don't throw anything out! You can recycle scrap paper, cardboard, yarn, string, and fabric to make collages. Plastic containers and glass jars are useful for mixing paint and cleaning brushes. Newspaper keeps your table clean, and you can cut it up or tear it to use in your pictures!

A camera

There's plenty you can do with photos in art (see pages 28–29). Digital cameras help you make exciting computer-enhanced art. Disposable cameras are cheap and light to carry around for spontaneous snapshots!

BE CAREFUL!

You can do most of the projects in this book on your own. For some, you will need an adult to help. The project instructions will tell you when you need to stop and ask for help.

pencils

sequins

scissors

Hints and tips

A well-organized work station will help you create great art. Find a corner where you can work undisturbed. Give yourself plenty of room to avoid spills and accidents.

Be prepared

Before you start, read through the project and check that you have everything you need. Cover your work surface with newspaper and your clothes with an apron or old shirt— some of the projects can be messy!

Getting ideas

While each of the projects in the book shows you how to achieve a different effect, you will get lots more ideas if you experiment on your own. Test the different effects on scrap paper, and label your results.

Keep an idea scrapbook to hold magazine clippings, wallpaper samples, photos—anything that inspires you!

Collect things!

Become a recycling expert. Always look out for things to you can use—or reuse! if you are out hiking, bring back grass, leaves, and flowers. Keep old toys, buttons, beads, and ribbons to use in collages, and raid the kitchen for dried pasta or beans (but ask first).

Taking the extra step

The special effects in this book make great artwork, and after you know how to use them, you can mix and match for even more amazing effects. For example, cut up a straw painting and use it in a collage or as the **background** for another painting. Take a bark rubbing made with crayon and use it as the basis for a wax resist print.

TIP

A sketchbook will help you keep track of your ideas and inspirations. Carry a small sketchbook with you so you can make quick drawings or jot down notes for future projects.

The artist chose an underwater theme for the frame of this mirror.

Using your artwork

Many of the special effects in this book can be used to make stunning homemade stationery. Any of the ideas would make wonderful greeting cards. Collage is ideal for covering picture frames or as a decorative mirror frame.

Don't throw away spare dripping and dabbing pictures (pages 10-11) or other decorated paper! Use them to make gift tags or envelopes.

Frame it

Choose your best work to frame, and start your own gallery on the walls of your room. Frames can be simple cardboard borders or wild and wacky shapes. You could even continue the pattern of your picture on the frame.

If you run out of space on your wall, you can keep favorite works of art in a folder made of two large pieces of cardboard threaded together.

Straw painting

You can create all kinds of beautiful and mysterious paint effects just by blowing paint through a straw. The results will be different every time!

WHAT YOU NEED

- Straws
- Bright poster paints
- Brushes
- Smooth paper

Did you know you can make paintings with a straw? Use this effect to create weird and wonderful images.

1 Mix up some watery paint. Use a brush to put two large blobs of paint onto the paper. Using the straw, blow the paint over the paper to make wiggly lines.

2 Let the first color dry. Repeat with different colors if you wish. Does the shape look like anything?

Guess the shape

When you make straw paintings, it is fun to start without knowing what picture you are going to create. Just start moving the paint around and wait for a shape to start appearing.

As you work, you will get ideas for what your picture could be. For example, this yellow burst just needed legs, eyes, and a beak to become a fuzzy chick! Use the straw technique as part of a traditional painting to create hair, a lion's mane, or tree branches.

TIP

Straw painting is great for making starry skies. Just use lots of small blobs of paint and blow genty on them.

Dripping and dabbing

Add blobs of paint or ink to wet paper to make stunning patterns and paintings. You can even use felt-tip markers or food dye!

WHAT YOU NEED
- Heavyweight paper
- Brushes
- Poster paint or colored ink

1 Tape the paper to a piece of cardboard to keep it from wrinkling. Wet the paper with a large brush dipped in water.

2 To make the petals of an open flower, drip blobs of paint in a circle. Single blobs make good flower buds. Let the paint spread and dry.

3 Use a thin brush to add leaves, stems, and other details.

4 Add a soft color as a background. Let water drop onto the paint to make a dappled effect.

TIP

Experiment with different watery paint effects. What happens when you add a blob of paint to another color that is still wet? Try some different colors.

Wax resist

Waxy crayons and watery paints don't mix—which means that if you draw a picture in crayon and then paint over the top, the drawing will show through.

1 Use the wax crayon to draw the outline of a squash and add some lines running along it.

2 Paint yellow paint over the wax. The wax will resist the paint, and the drawing will show through.

3 Let the yellow paint dry. It will settle between the wax lines.

4 When the yellow paint is dry, add some more wax lines.

5 Add green paint. The wax allows the yellow to show through.

Scratchboard

While watery paints slide off wax crayon, you can get quite different results if you cover the whole area with thick paint, and then scrape patterns on the surface.

WHAT YOU NEED
- Heavyweight paper or posterboard
- Crayons or a candle
- Poster paint • Brushes

Make your own scratchboard art

1 Cover the paper with crayon, without any gaps. Whatever color you use will show through, so choose bright colors or white.

2 Now brush thick, black paint over the crayon surface, and let it dry. Repeat two or three times until the crayon is completely covered.

3 Scratch a pattern in the surface, using various tools. Try the end of a paintbrush, a popsicle stick, or a knitting needle.

TIP

Experiment with different scratchboard techniques. Instead of using light-colored crayon with black paint, use dark crayons and white paint—black showing through white is very dramatic.

TIP

You could also try making lots of small scratchboard pictures rather than one large one. Or try using lots of different colors of crayon—diagonal lines of red and orange make great flickering flames.

Wax transfer

You can use wax crayons to make homemade transfers. Try out some simple designs, such as flower shapes. Once you have practiced this technique, go on to make more detailed, colorful pictures.

1 Cover part of a piece of paper with heavy crayon. Lay a clean piece of paper on top.

2 Draw a simple design on top of the paper with the pencil. Fill it in, pressing hard.

3 Lift off the paper. The crayon should have transferred to the underside of the top piece of paper, leaving a pale copy on the piece below.

Color transfer

Using this wax transfer effect, you can turn a simple **silhouette** into an unusual and colorful picture.

WHAT YOU NEED
- A sheet of parchment paper
- Heavyweight paper
- Crayons
- A pencil

1 Lightly draw or trace a design on one side of the parchment paper. You don't need to keep the shapes simple.

2 Turn the parchment paper over, and color it with different colors of crayons. Try bands of color, splotches, circles, or squares.

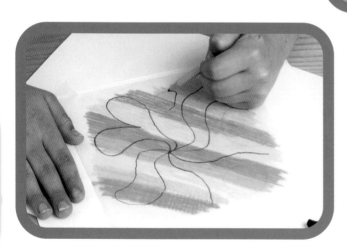

3 Place the paper, crayon-side down, on a clean sheet of paper. Tape the edges so it doesn't slip. Now go over all the lines and areas of solid color with the pencil, pressing firmly.

4 Lift off the parchment paper to see the wax transfer beneath.

Glitter glue

Glitter comes in lots of different colors and can be used to make wonderful, sparkling pictures. Try this cool idea!

Paint and sparkle

In this project, you use glue like paint to draw the shapes you want in your picture. Before the glue is dry, add some sparkle!

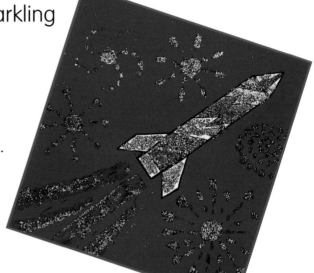

WHAT YOU NEED
- Paper
- Pencil
- Glitter
- Glue
- Brush

A picture of outer space gets a lift from glitter glue. What other subjects would look good with a little glitz?

1 Draw the outline of the shapes in your picture in pencil. These are just guides for the glue stage.

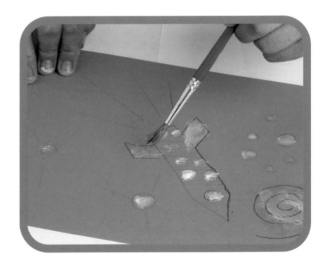

2 Use the brush to put glue wherever you want glitter. Leave it in blobs or fill in the shapes you drew.

3 Before the glue dries, sprinkle glitter onto the picture. Use different colored glitters for different areas so the finished picture is bright. Leave the glitter on for a few minutes, then blow genty to remove any loose pieces. (This gets messy, so make sure to protect things you don't want sprinkled with glitter!) Now, stand back and admire!

TIP

You can make your own glitter paint. Just mix some glitter with some glue and use a brush to put the sparkly paint on your paper. Now you can make your own glittering masterpieces.

Fabric collage

So far, the art projects in this book have used paints, crayons, and inks. Did you know that you can also make fantastic pictures using fabric?

A material world

Using fabric to make a picture helps to make lots of interesting textures and shapes. Try this country scene.

1 First, sketch the outlines of the scene in soft pencil. It is best to use cardboard, because normal paper might tear with lots of heavy fabric on it.

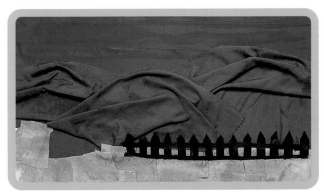

2 Cut out fabric for the background. We used blue for the sky, dark green for hills, and light green for the fields. Glue them in place.

3 Now start adding details, such as a fence, a hedge, trees, animals in the fields, clouds, and some flowers.

TIP

Old pieces of fabric come in handy for this project. Scraps of white lace are excellent for making clouds or snowy scenes. Ribbons are good for creating flowers. Experiment with different fabrics for making different objects.

TIP

When you have finished your fabric collage, you can paint it with clear varnish. This adds depth and makes the surface of the picture shine. The varnish effect looks especially nice on a dark background.

Paper sewing

Sewing isn't just for fabric. You can also use a needle and thread to make great designs on paper or cardboard. Always ask an adult for help when you want to use a needle. You could even use sewing to add pizzazz to a traditional painting!

Embroidery house

This simple project will show you the basic method of paper sewing. Try some other designs, too.

1 Tape a piece of paper with a simple design onto the posterboard. Sew in and out through the paper and board. When you finish with a color, cut the thread, leaving long tails hanging loose at both ends.

2 On the back of the posterboard, knot the ends of the loose threads, and cut the ends short. Put tape over the threads to hold them securely. Gently remove the paper from the front.

3 Cut another piece of posterboard slightly larger than your picture. Glue the sewing picture onto this.

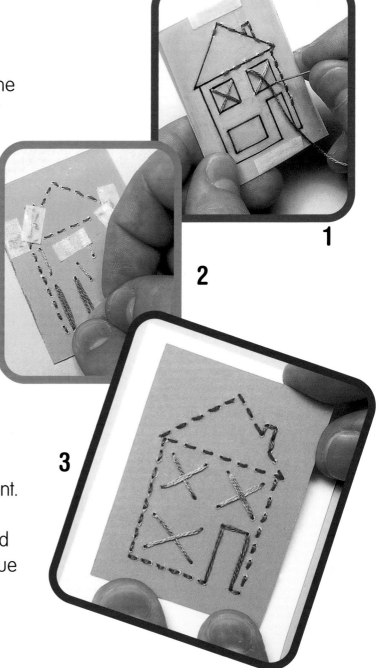

1

2

3

Stitching decorations

There a lots of variations you can use with paper sewing. Try putting colorful beads onto the thread and making zigzag patterns. Use thread to make decorative borders on your cards and letters. Just make sure you use thick enough paper to hold the thread.

Paper pricking

You can also decorate a picture using just a needle to poke holes. The holes will show up nicely when light shines through them. This is a technique called paper pricking.

TIP

See if you can use sewing in some of your paintings or collages. You could use thread to make hair, colorful plants in the garden, or even a waterfall. Use different colors of thread together for interesting results.

As well as decorative borders, you can use sewing to make colorful designs for birthday and Christmas cards. Using the same method as the project on page 22, you can make any shape or design you like.

Collage

Paper and cardboard are cheap, colorful, and easy to cut and paste, which makes it perfect for collage. Collect as many scraps as you can find—you never know when they may come in handy!

WHAT YOU NEED
- Colored paper
- Magazines
- Posterboard or cardboard
- Glue

Making a collage

1 Sketch out a design on cardboard or posterboard.

2 Cut or tear paper into interesting shapes.

3 Arrange the shapes until you are happy with the way they look, and glue them in place.

Mosaic

Try some different techniques in your collages. What about cutting out lots of small, colored squares from old magazines and making them into an image like a Roman **mosaic**?

Experiment with other materials, too, such as buttons, kitchen foil, and newspaper. You could also paint bits of paper different colors, tear them up, and then use them in your collages. Torn paper creates interesting textures.

Here is another colorful collage made with different types of paper.

You can tear paper into the shapes of animals, flowers, and trees.

TIP

Once you have used paper to make colorful collages, you can go on to make paper **sculptures**! Cut out the shapes you'll need for your design, then color them before you glue them together. You can make hair by cutting thin strips of paper.

Check out this crazy paper sculpture!

Extra materials

Odds and ends from around the home look great in collages: fabric, lace, ribbons, sequins, pasta, beans, and toothpicks. You could probably make a collage from the contents of your wastepaper basket!

WHAT YOU NEED

- Feathers
- String
- Toothpicks
- Colored paper
- Dry leaves
- Beads
- Rice
- Cardboard

Perfect pets

1 Draw the outline of your favorite animal with a pen, and cut it out. Cut out other shapes, such as grass and clouds, to make a scene.

2 Arrange the shapes on the cardboard. When you are happy with the way they look, glue them down.

3 Now use the other odds and ends to finish the scene. We used a bead for the eye, rice for flowers, toothpicks and string for the fence, colored paper for the apples, and feathers for the mane and tail.

Still life

All the ingredients in this collage are easy to find. You can personalize it by mixing the collage with painting and adding other natural materials, such as dried beans, seeds, and pasta.

1 Look at the items you've collected and think how you could make them into a collage. Sketch the design on a piece of cardboard.

2 Arrange your collection on the pencil outline. Glue the pieces in place.

3 You could leave your collage as it is. Or use paint add more flowers or a background for your picture. Try adding color to some of the objects in the collage if you like.

Using photos

A camera can be useful for making art. You can get all kinds of unusual effects if you combine photos with painting and collage. Take your own photos, or cut your favorites from magazines.

Fantasy fun

1 Want a different home? Take a photo of your house and paint an unusual background to make it look as if you live somewhere different. Look in travel brochures for inspiration.

2 Cut out the house and glue it to the background, or **superimpose** it using computer software. Send it as a postcard to family or friends.

3 What about adding a friend or a pet to your picture? You could have fun playing with size and **proportion**, too! In your fantasy picture, objects can be as big or small as you like.

Picture strips

1 Find two photos, roughly the same size. Using a ruler and a pen, make lines ¾ inch apart across each photo.

2 Cut along the lines to make neat strips.

3 Glue the first strip from the first picture onto some cardboard, followed by the first strip from the second picture. Keep trading off until you've used all the strips.

You can use this effect to mix different animals, or alternate photos of an animal and a person or a landscape.

Try cutting the strips diagonally and horizontally, too.

Glossary

background   the area of a picture behind the main object—for example, a field and distant hills

collage   making pictures or patterns using different materials such as paper, cloth, and photographs, which are glued onto a background.

embroidery   making pictures or patterns with sewing

mosaic   a picture made up of lots of small squares of color

proportion   the size of one thing compared to the size of something else

sculptures   art made by carving or constructing objects

sequins   small, shiny pieces of metal or plastic, often used in sparkly dresses

silhouette   when an object is seen against a light background, with just the outline visible

superimpose   to put one thing on top of another

texture   the way something feels—for example, it could be rough or smooth

Index

backgrounds 6, 11, 27, 28, 30
bark rubbings 6
beads 23
beans 27
blowing paint 8–9
brushes 4, 5
    cleaning 4–5
buttons 25

cameras 5, 28
candles 4, 13
cards 23
chalk pastels 5
collage 4, 5, 6, 7, 20, 21, 23, 28, 30;
    materials 5, 26–27
    paper 24–25
collecting 6
computers 5, 28
crayons 4, 12, 13

dabbing 7, 10–11
dappled effect 11
digital cameras 5
dripping 7, 10–11

embroidery 22, 30
extra materials 4–5, 26–27

fabric 26

felt-tip pens 10
flowers, blurry effect 10–11
food dye 10
frames 7

glitter project 18–19
greeting cards 23

ideas 6
inks 4

lace 26

magazines 25, 28, 29
materials 4–5, 26–27
mirror frames 7
mosaics 25, 30

newspaper 25

paints 4
paper 4
    wrinkled 10
paper collage 24–25
paper pricking 23
paper sewing 22–23
pasta 6, 26
pets picture 26
photos 28–29
picture frames 7
picture strips 29

postcards 28
poster paints 4

ribbon 23

scrapbook 6, 16
scratchboard art 4, 14–15
seeds 27
sequins 26, 30
sewing 22–23
silhouettes 17, 30
sketchbook 6
stationery 7
still life 27
straw painting 8–9
straws 4, 8, 20
superimposing 28, 30

texture 4, 30
textured paper 4
thread 22, 23
tools 4, 4–5, 14, 26
torn paper 25
transfers 16–17
travel brochures 28

wax crayons 4, 5, 12, 13, 16, 17
wax resist 12–13
wax transfer 4, 16–17
wet paper technique 10–11

Notes to teachers and parents

The projects in this book can be used as home projects or as part of an art class. The ideas offer children inspiration, but you should always encourage them to draw from their own imagination and first-hand observation, as well as from memory and their own different experiences.

Sourcing ideas

All art projects should tap into children's interests, and be relevant to their lives and experiences. Some stimulating starting points include found objects, discussions about their family and pets, hobbies, TV shows, or current affairs.

Encourage children to source their own ideas and references, from books, magazines, or the Internet. Digital cameras can create reference material (pictures of landscapes, people, or animals) that can be printed out later to look at while drawing.

Other lessons can often be an ideal springboard for an art project—for example, an investigation into your local area could result in a class collage, a field trip could yield rubbings for a wax and resist project, and mosaics work well with ancient history projects.

Encourage children to keep a sketchbook of their ideas, and to collect images and objects to help them develop their art.

Give pupils as many first-hand experiences as possible through visits and contact with creative people.

Evaluating work

It's important and motivating for children to share their work with others, and to compare ideas and methods. Encourage them to talk about their work. What do they like best about it? How would they do it differently next time?

Show the children examples of other artists' work. How did they tackle the same subject and problems? Do the children like the work? Why or why not?

Help children recognize the originality and value of their work, to appreciate the different qualities in others' work, and to respect ways of working that are different from their own. Display children's work for all to admire!

Expanding the techniques

Look at ways to develop extensions to a project. For example, many of the ideas in this book could be adapted for painting, collage, and printmaking. You can use image-enhancing computer software and digital scanners to enhance, build up, and juxtapose images.

Help your artist(s) set up an art gallery to show off their work, or scan artwork and post the images to a photo website where others can log in and view them. Having their work displayed professionally will make them feel that their work is valued.